ANIMALS AT A GLANCE
HOUSE PETS

OJ DP AR MC VWM

For a free color catalog describing Gareth Stevens' list of high-quality books, call 1-800-542-2595 (USA) or 1-800-461-9120 (Canada). Gareth Stevens' Fax: (414) 225-0377.

The editor would like to thank Elizabeth S. Frank, Curator of Large Mammals at the Milwaukee County Zoo, Milwaukee, Wisconsin, for her kind and professional assistance regarding the accuracy of the information in this book.

Library of Congress Cataloging-in-Publication Data

Dudek, Isabella.
   [Haustiere. English]
   House pets / by Isabella Dudek ; illustrated by Heinrich Kita.
      p. cm. -- (Animals at a glance)
   Includes index.
   ISBN 0-8368-1357-X
   1. Pets--Juvenile literature. [1. Pets.] I. Kita, Heinrich,
ill. II. Title. III. Series: Lerne Tiere kennen. English.
SF416.2.D8313 1995
636.088'7--dc20   95-13963

This edition first published in 1996 by
Gareth Stevens Publishing
1555 North RiverCenter Drive, Suite 201
Milwaukee, Wisconsin 53212, USA

This edition © 1996 by Gareth Stevens, Inc. Original edition published in 1991 by Mangold Verlag, LDV Datenverarbeitung Gesellschaft m.b.H., A8042 Graz, St-Peter-Hauptstrasse 28, Austria, under the title **Lerne Tiere Kennen-Haustiere**. Text © 1991 by Isabella Dudek. Illustrations © 1991 by Heinrich Kita. Additional end matter © 1996 by Gareth Stevens, Inc.

Series editor: Barbara J. Behm
Editorial assistants: Diana L. Kahn, Diane Laska
Logo Design: Helene Feider

Printed in Mexico

1 2 3 4 5 6 7 8 9 99 98 97 96

ANIMALS AT A GLANCE
HOUSE PETS

by ISABELLA DUDEK
Illustrated by HEINRICH KITA

Hooked bill

Parakeets are small to medium-sized parrots

Brightly colored

Short legs

PARAKEETS

Long, pointed tail

Gareth Stevens Publishing
MILWAUKEE

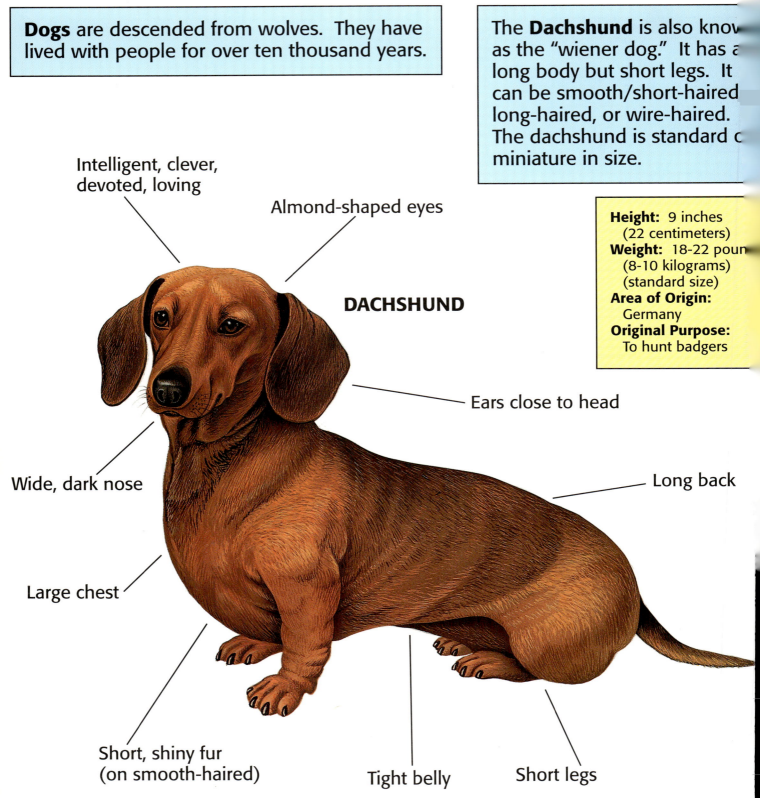

Dogs are descended from wolves. They have lived with people for over ten thousand years.

The **Dachshund** is also know[n] as the "wiener dog." It has a long body but short legs. It can be smooth/short-haired, long-haired, or wire-haired. The dachshund is standard o[r] miniature in size.

Height: 9 inches
(22 centimeters)
Weight: 18-22 poun[ds]
(8-10 kilograms)
(standard size)
Area of Origin:
Germany
Original Purpose:
To hunt badgers

Intelligent, clever, devoted, loving

Almond-shaped eyes

DACHSHUND

Ears close to head

Wide, dark nose

Long back

Large chest

Short, shiny fur
(on smooth-haired)

Tight belly

Short legs

4

Intelligent, alert, playful

e **Poodle** usually s a curly coat in a id color. It can be standard, miniature, toy size.

Height: 15 inches (38 cm)
Weight: 20 pounds (9 kg)
  (miniature size)
Area of Origin:
  France, Germany
Original Purpose: To
  retrieve from water

Long ears that widen at bottom

Dogs see in black and white only

Thick hair

Dogs' sense of smell is thirty times greater than humans'

needs ar grooming

Straight legs

Arched toes

Small paws

POODLE

5

Height: 15-16 inches (38-41 cm)
Weight: 29-32 pounds (13-14.5 kg)
Area of Origin: From Spain to England; specific kind developed in the United States
Original Purpose: To retrieve birds on land and in water

The **Cocker spaniel** is one of the smalle[st] sporting dogs. It w[as] named for its skill a[t] hunting a bird calle[d] the woodcock.

Wide, sensitive nos[e]

Gentle, loving

Long, droopy ears

Cockers come in solid colors or two/three tones

Wavy, silky hair

Small, thickly padded paws

Round skull, round eyes

Puppies are born in groups called litters

COCKER SPANIEL

6

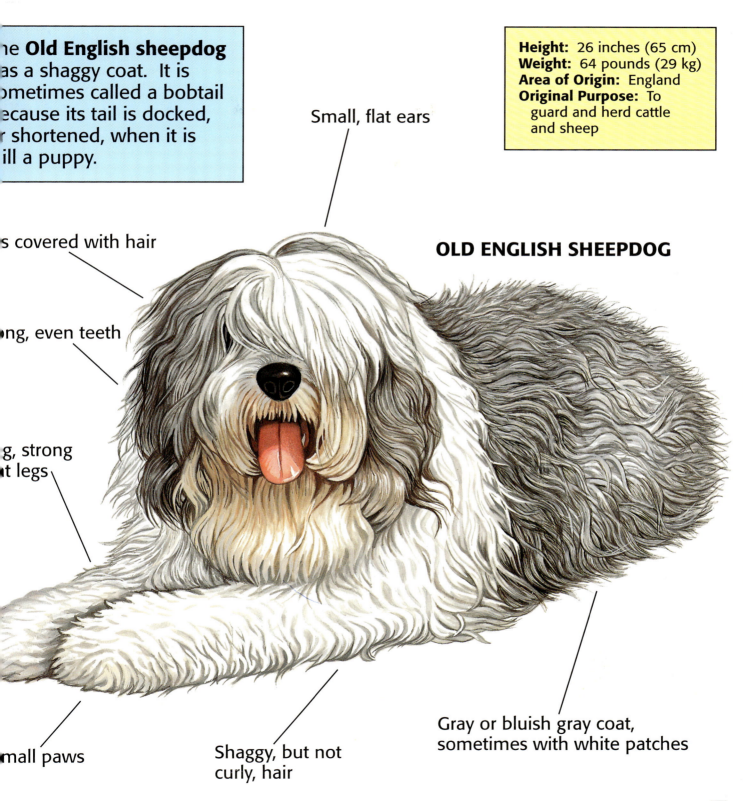

The **Old English sheepdog** ~~h~~as a shaggy coat. It is ~~s~~ometimes called a bobtail ~~b~~ecause its tail is docked, ~~o~~r shortened, when it is ~~st~~ill a puppy.

Height: 26 inches (65 cm)
Weight: 64 pounds (29 kg)
Area of Origin: England
Original Purpose: To guard and herd cattle and sheep

Small, flat ears

OLD ENGLISH SHEEPDOG

~~Eye~~s covered with hair

~~Stro~~ng, even teeth

~~Lon~~g, strong ~~fron~~t legs

Gray or bluish gray coat, sometimes with white patches

~~S~~mall paws

Shaggy, but not curly, hair

7

Length: 18 inches (46 cm)
Weight: 4-18 pounds (1.8-8.2 kg)
Area of Origin: North Africa, Egypt
Original Purpose: To catch rats and mice

The **House cat** descended from th North African wildcat. There are ov thirty different breeds of house cat in existence. The ancient Egyptian regarded the cat as a holy animal.

Can see six times better than humans

Can be sh haired, lor haired, or curly-haire

Jumps long and high

HOUSE CAT

Pulls claws in when walking

Kittens separate from mothers at 2 months old

Kittens are very playful

Usually 4 kittens in a litter

Can live to be fifteen or more years old

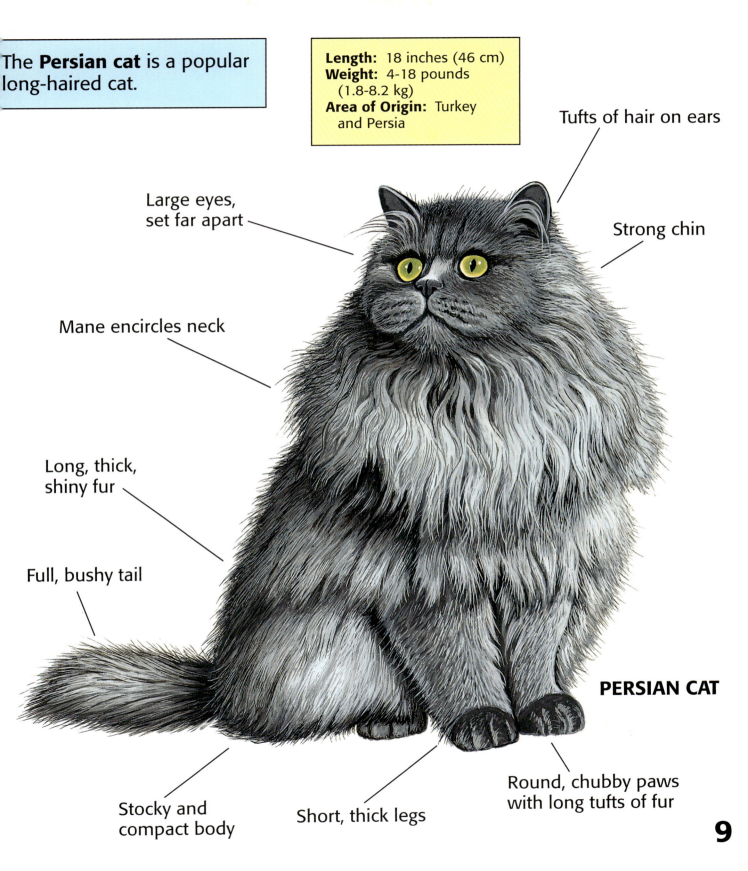

The **Persian cat** is a popular long-haired cat.

Length: 18 inches (46 cm)
Weight: 4-18 pounds (1.8-8.2 kg)
Area of Origin: Turkey and Persia

Tufts of hair on ears

Strong chin

Large eyes, set far apart

Mane encircles neck

Long, thick, shiny fur

Full, bushy tail

Stocky and compact body

Short, thick legs

Round, chubby paws with long tufts of fur

PERSIAN CAT

9

The **Siamese cat** is slender and short-haired. It has blue eyes. It is a great leaper and is very vocal.

Length: 18 inches (46 c
Weight: 4-18 pounds
(1.8-8.2 kg)
Area of Origin: Thailan
(formerly Siam)

Large, slanted eyes

Small, triangular nose

Large, pointed ears

Long, thin neck

Strong muscles

Short, shiny crea
colored fur with
darker color on
face, legs, and ta

SIAMESE CAT

Small, oval paws

10 Long, thin, pointed tail

The **Parrot** family includes the macaws, parakeets, and cockatoos. There are more than three hundred types. Some parrots have become extinct, and care should be taken not to take part in activities that would harm endangered birds, such as purchasing them or hunting them. Never purchase birds that are caught in the wild; only purchase those that are bred in captivity as house pets.

Length: 3.5-40 inches (9-102 cm)
Country of Origin: mainly Central and South America, Australia, Malaysia, Philippines
Diet: Plants, fruits, nuts, seeds, pollen, nectar, vegetables, roots

Eats, climbs, and digs with curved beak

Good eyesight

Good hearing

Some mimic words and sounds

PARAKEETS

The **Parakeet** is a beautifully colored, slender parrot that has a long tail.

Two front toes, two back toes

Length: 8-16 inches (20.3-40.6 cm)
Area of Origin: Australia
Diet: Fruits and seeds

Straight, thin tail

11

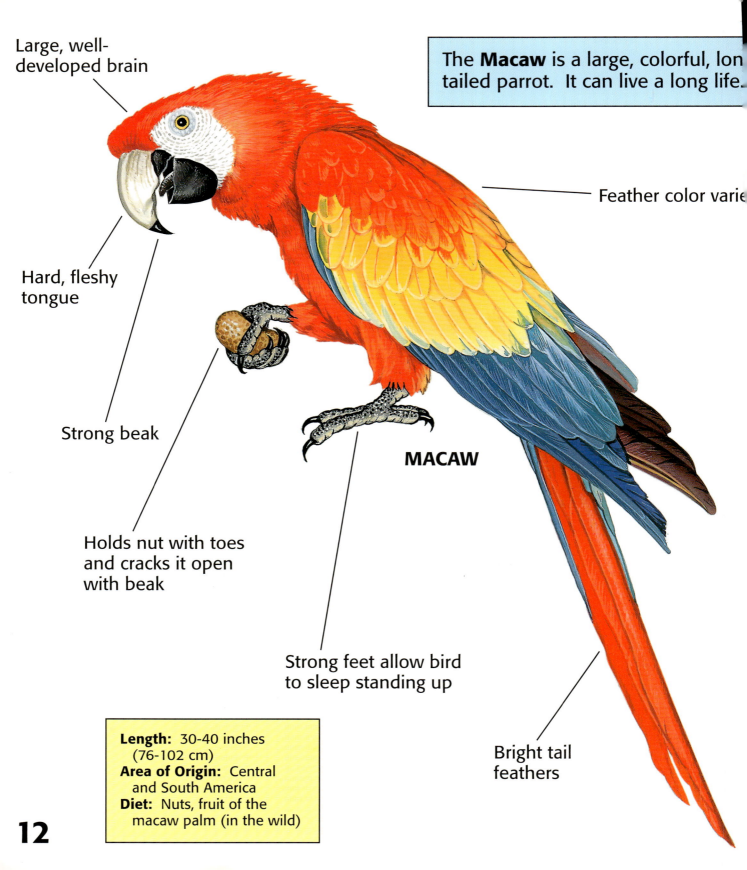

Large, well-developed brain

The **Macaw** is a large, colorful, lon[g]-tailed parrot. It can live a long life.

Feather color varie[s]

Hard, fleshy tongue

Strong beak

Holds nut with toes and cracks it open with beak

MACAW

Strong feet allow bird to sleep standing up

Bright tail feathers

Length: 30-40 inches (76-102 cm)
Area of Origin: Central and South America
Diet: Nuts, fruit of the macaw palm (in the wild)

12

e **Cockatoo** is a parrot
t is mainly white in color.

Length: 13-20 inches (33-51 cm)
Area of Origin: Malaysia to Australia
  to the Philippines
Diet: Nuts, fruits, vegetables, and roots

The **Amazon parrot** is a blue-headed parrot. There are 27 different types. The Amazon parrot is the type of parrot most often kept as a pet.

Length: 15 inches (38 cm)
Area of Origin: South America
Diet: Fruits, seeds

Crest stands
straight up

igent, talks

erful beak

Feathers replace
themselves

Bright blue
forehead

AMAZON PARROT

Lays 2-5 eggs

COCKATOO

13

The **Canary** that is kept as a pet was developed from the wild canary. It is popular for its beautiful singing.

Length: 4-9 inches (10-23 cm)
Area of Origin: Canary Islands, Africa
Diet: Seeds, greens

Short, strong beak

Tame canaries come in many colors. But in the wild, they are olive green.

Adults teach their young to sing

Round eyes

Overlapping feathers

Tiny legs

CANARIES

Forked tail feathers

One toe in back

Three toes in front

The **Finch** belongs to the sparrow family. There are over 120 kinds of finches in the wild.

Length: 4-6 inches (10-15 cm)
Area of Origin: Africa, Australia, South America
Diet: Seeds

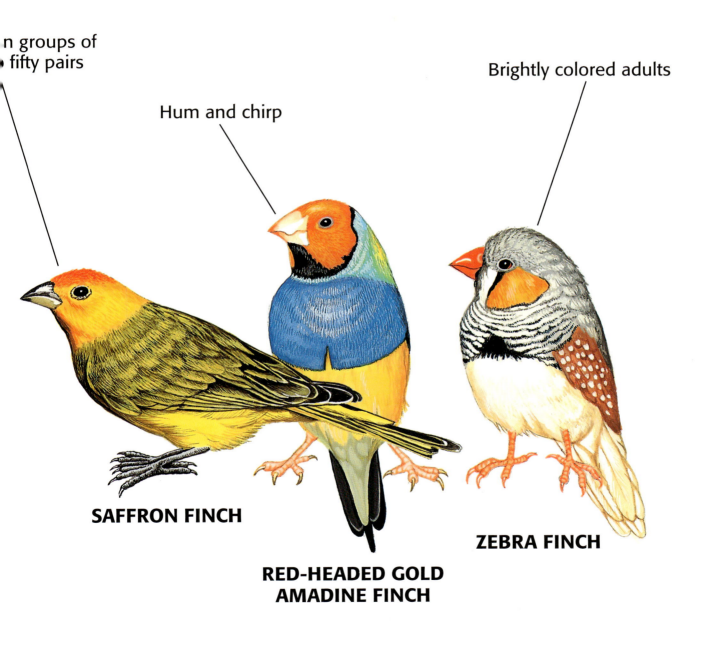

n groups of
fifty pairs

Hum and chirp

Brightly colored adults

SAFFRON FINCH

RED-HEADED GOLD AMADINE FINCH

ZEBRA FINCH

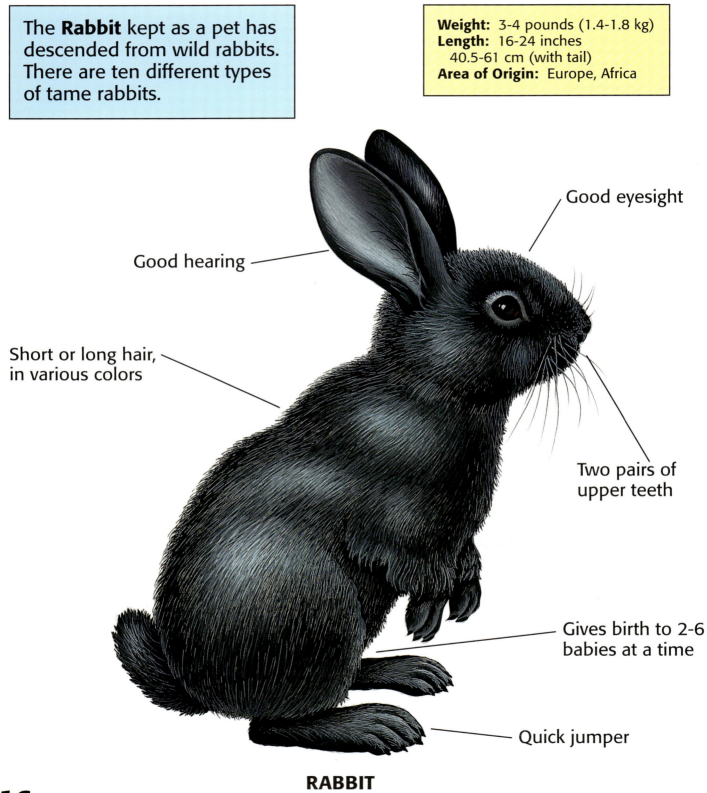

The **Rabbit** kept as a pet has descended from wild rabbits. There are ten different types of tame rabbits.

Weight: 3-4 pounds (1.4-1.8 kg)
Length: 16-24 inches
40.5-61 cm (with tail)
Area of Origin: Europe, Africa

Good eyesight

Good hearing

Short or long hair, in various colors

Two pairs of upper teeth

Gives birth to 2-6 babies at a time

Quick jumper

RABBIT

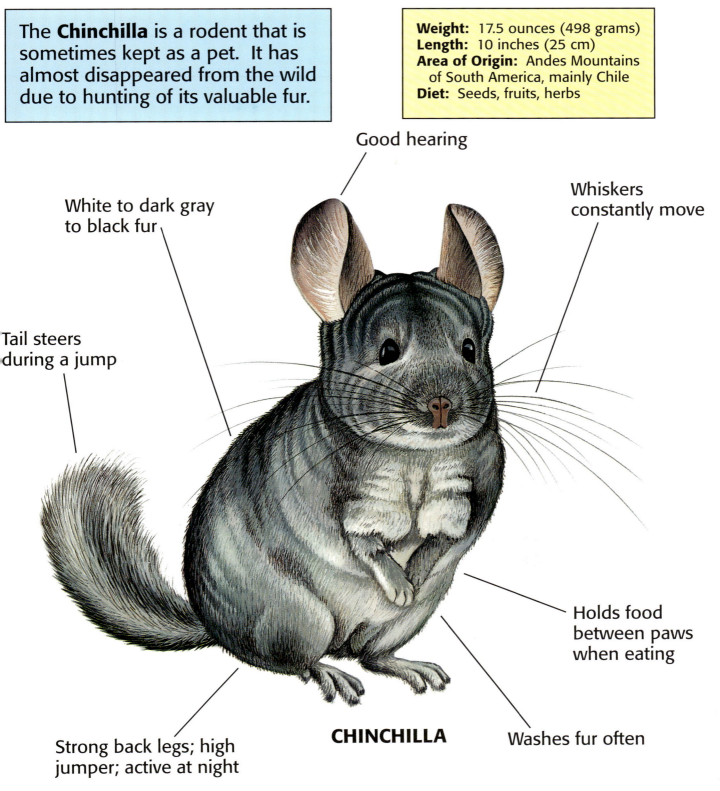

The **Chinchilla** is a rodent that is sometimes kept as a pet. It has almost disappeared from the wild due to hunting of its valuable fur.

Weight: 17.5 ounces (498 grams)
Length: 10 inches (25 cm)
Area of Origin: Andes Mountains of South America, mainly Chile
Diet: Seeds, fruits, herbs

Good hearing

Whiskers constantly move

White to dark gray to black fur

Tail steers during a jump

Holds food between paws when eating

CHINCHILLA

Strong back legs; high jumper; active at night

Washes fur often

The **Guinea pig** comes in many different colors. It is a rodent.

Weight: 3 pounds (1.4 kg)
Length: 12 inches (30 cm)
Area of Origin: South America
Diet: Plant matter

Grunts, mumbles, and whistles

Good hearing

Thick, shiny coat

Knows family by sense of smell

Whiskers guide it in the dark

Claws be trim

1-4 babies in a litter

GUINEA PIG

18

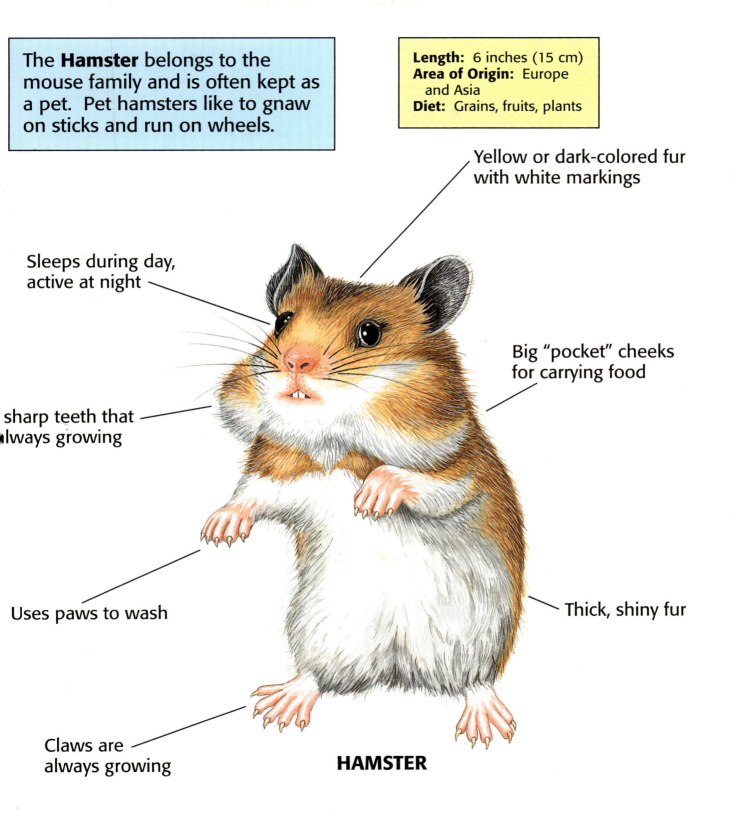

The **Hamster** belongs to the mouse family and is often kept as a pet. Pet hamsters like to gnaw on sticks and run on wheels.

Length: 6 inches (15 cm)
Area of Origin: Europe and Asia
Diet: Grains, fruits, plants

Yellow or dark-colored fur with white markings

Sleeps during day, active at night

sharp teeth that always growing

Big "pocket" cheeks for carrying food

Uses paws to wash

Thick, shiny fur

Claws are always growing

HAMSTER

19

Washes its face with paws

Gerbils and **Mice** come in many different colors. They mark their home with a scent. They have 3-8 babies at a time.

Weight: 4 ounces (113 g)
Length: 4 inches (10.2 cm)
Area of Origin: Mice and most gerbils – Africa, Asia, and Middle East; Mongolian gerbil – Mongolia
Diet: Plants, seeds

Long, furry tail

Stands and jumps

MONGOLIAN GERBIL

Newborns soon grow fur

Live in groups

BLACK MOUSE

BROWN MOUSE

WHITE MOUSE

rtles and **Tortoises**
e reptiles.

When frightened, pulls itself inside shell

Weight: up to 13 pounds (6 kg)
Length: 10 inches (25 cm)
Area of Origin: Spain and Portugal
Diet: Plants, some meat

blooded; body
erature is the
e as the air

Intelligent; can learn

arious skin
atterns

od sense
smell

Lives on land

TORTOISE

g, sharp jaws;
eat some meat

TURTLE

is made
ne

Lives on land
and in water

Webbed toes; good
swimmer, digger, and walker

21

The **Salamander** lives on damp land or in water of the northern parts of the world. Salamanders are amphibians with tails. There are about 350 different kinds.

Length: 5-12 inches (12.7-30.5 cm)
Area of Origin: North America, Mexico, China, Japan
Diet: Insects

Bright color acts as a warning to animals

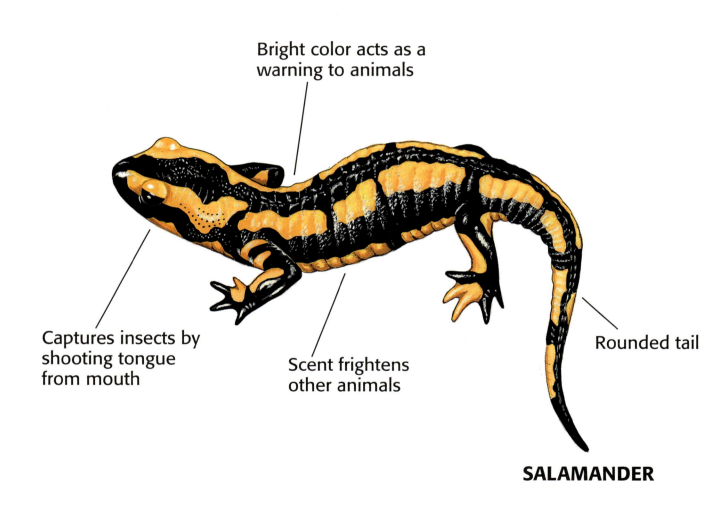

Captures insects by shooting tongue from mouth

Scent frightens other animals

Rounded tail

SALAMANDER

The **Frog** is an amphibian that lives in grass and water. There are 250 different species.

Length: 2-4 inches (5-10 cm)
Area of Origin: North America, South America, Africa, Europe, Asia
Diet: Insects

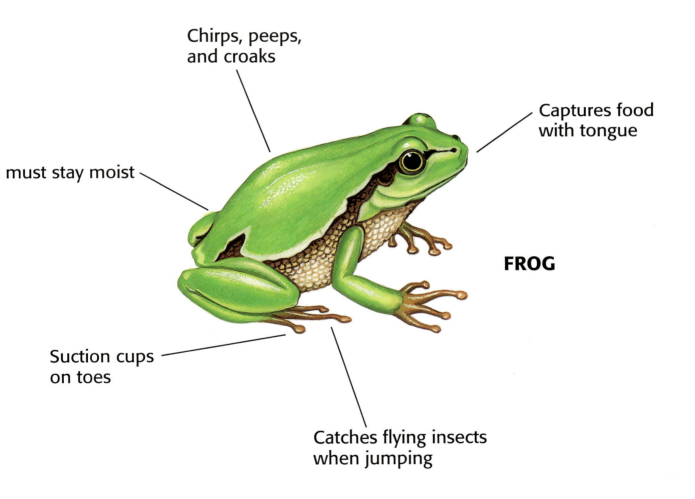

Chirps, peeps, and croaks

Captures food with tongue

must stay moist

Suction cups on toes

FROG

Catches flying insects when jumping

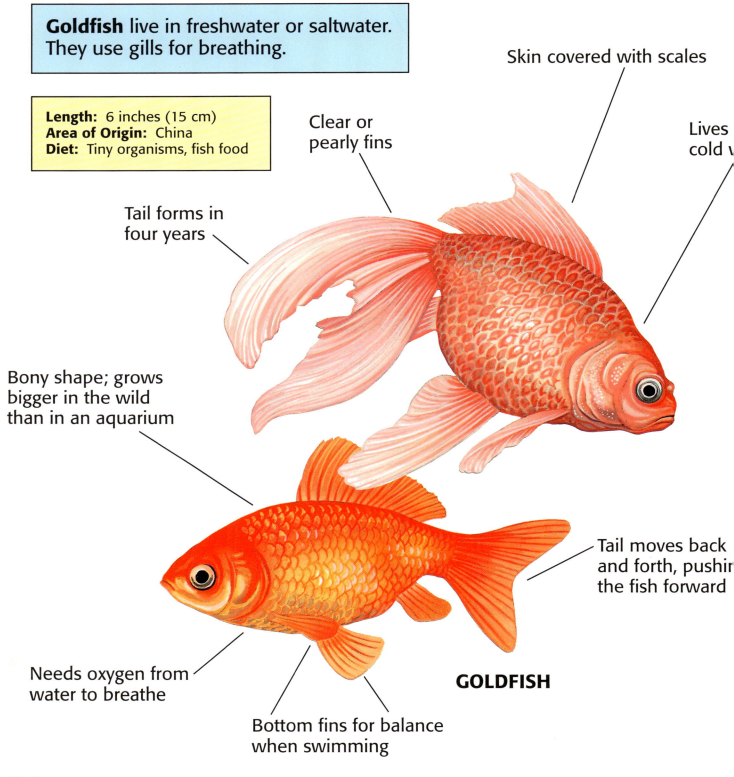

Goldfish live in freshwater or saltwater. They use gills for breathing.

Length: 6 inches (15 cm)
Area of Origin: China
Diet: Tiny organisms, fish food

Skin covered with scales

Clear or pearly fins

Lives
cold v

Tail forms in four years

Bony shape; grows bigger in the wild than in an aquarium

Tail moves back and forth, pushir the fish forward

Needs oxygen from water to breathe

GOLDFISH

Bottom fins for balance when swimming

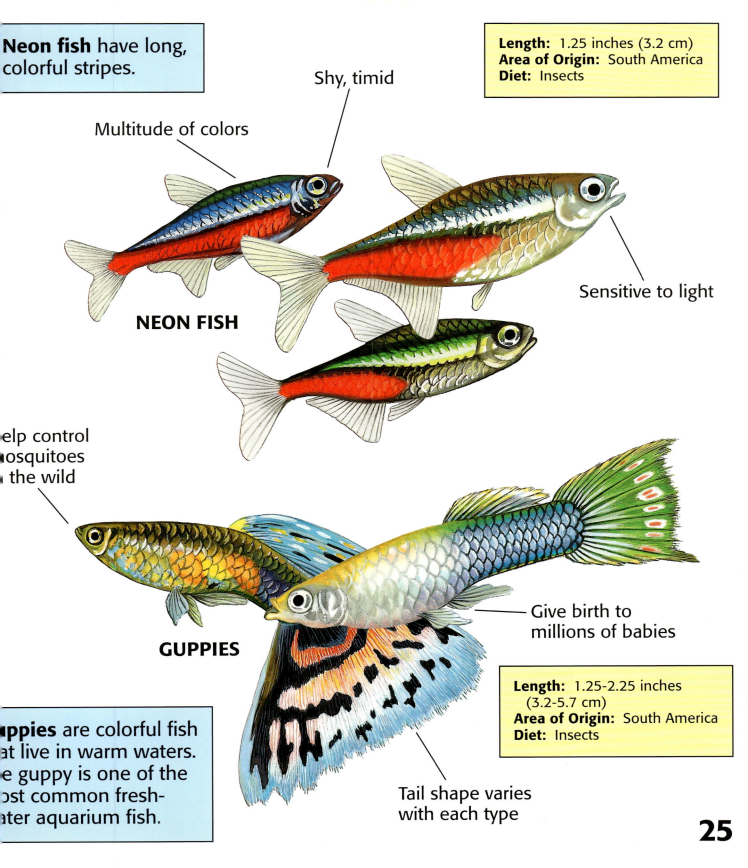

Neon fish have long, colorful stripes.

Multitude of colors

Shy, timid

Length: 1.25 inches (3.2 cm)
Area of Origin: South America
Diet: Insects

Sensitive to light

NEON FISH

Help control mosquitoes in the wild

Give birth to millions of babies

GUPPIES

Length: 1.25-2.25 inches (3.2-5.7 cm)
Area of Origin: South America
Diet: Insects

Guppies are colorful fish that live in warm waters. The guppy is one of the most common freshwater aquarium fish.

Tail shape varies with each type

25

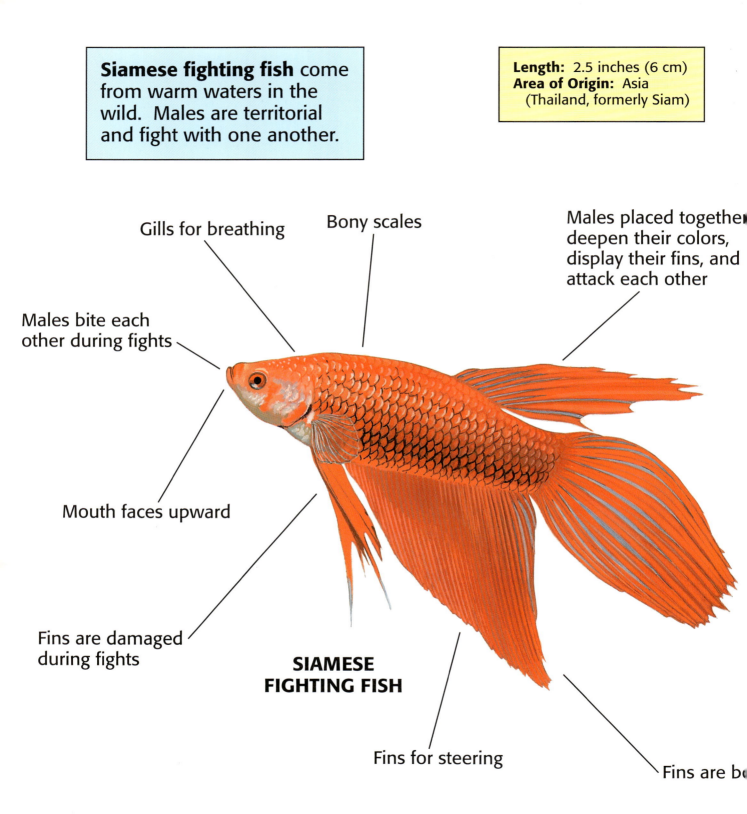

Siamese fighting fish come from warm waters in the wild. Males are territorial and fight with one another.

Length: 2.5 inches (6 cm)
Area of Origin: Asia (Thailand, formerly Siam)

Gills for breathing

Bony scales

Males placed together deepen their colors, display their fins, and attack each other

Males bite each other during fights

Mouth faces upward

Fins are damaged during fights

SIAMESE FIGHTING FISH

Fins for steering

Fins are b

ACTIVITIES

1. Call your local humane society to learn how to properly train your cat, dog, or other pet.

2. If you don't actually have a pet, do research to see what the appropriate pet for you might be. Consider your housing situation and home life.

3. Make up a story about an adventure that you and your pet have. Write the story down and illustrate it to create your own book!

4. Get some books from the library and learn more facts about the animals you might enjoy having as pets. Then write a play so that your friends can play the parts of the pets and owners. Make the play more realistic by creating costumes and scenery.

5. Create an aquarium or a terrarium from information you find at the library. Learn which animals could safely live in the habitats.

6. Visit a pet store. How many of the animals from this book do you see there?

7. Contact a state or national park to see if they have a nature program you can attend.

8. Volunteer or raise funds for your local or the national humane society.

FUN FACTS

1. The body temperature of a cold-blooded animal changes as the temperature of its surroundings changes.

2. Dogs are meat-eaters.

3. Cats in the wild are nocturnal – they hunt at night and sleep during the day.

4. Some goldfish can live to be fifty years old.

5. If goldfish live in rivers and streams, they lose their color.

6. The tortoise can live only on land.

7. The tortoise can live 100 years.

8. A rabbit can hop more than 10 feet (3 meters) in one hop and run about 18 miles (30 kilometers) per hour if afraid.

9. A mother rabbit uses fur from her own chest to cover her babies.

10. A baby rabbit is called a kit.

11. There are nine different breeds of sheepdogs around the world.

GLOSSARY

alert: watchful, ready.

amphibian: an animal that has a skeleton, is cold-blooded, can live in water and on land, and that develops lungs.

aquarium: a container of water used to provide living space for water animals and plants.

arched: curved.

beak: a bird's hard, pointed mouth.

descended: born of a certain source, an ancestry.

devoted: very loyal.

endangered: in danger of dying out, or becoming extinct.

extinct: no longer surviving on Earth.

fins: the thin, flat parts of a water animal's body that propel it through the water and balance it.

gills: the body parts of some water animals that are used for taking oxygen from the water for breathing.

litter: the offspring of a mother animal born in one delivery.

mimic: copy, imitate.

miniature: very small.

nectar: the sweet liquid found in many flowers.

oval: shaped like an egg.

pollen: the tiny grains of a flower that fertilize plants to produce seeds.

reptiles: a group of animals that creeps or crawls on the ground. Reptiles are cold-blooded, have backbones, and usually have scales.

retrieve: to bring back.

rodents: animals such as mice, rats, squirrels, and chinchillas that have large front teeth for gnawing.

scent: a particular smell or odor.

slanted: on a slope or incline.

solid: filled, firm.

sporting dog: a pointer, setter, or retriever – a dog that was originally bred and trained to hunt and track.

standard: regular size.

tame: domesticated, not wild.

territorial: very protective of one's home region.

tones: variations of the same color.

toy: a very small size; with regard to animal sizes, toy is smaller than miniature.

tuft: a bunch of hairs growing closely together.

wildcat: a small or medium-sized wild animal that is related to the house cat.

BOOKS TO READ

A First Look at Dogs. Millicent E. Selsam and Joyce Hunt (Walker)

A Look Through the Mousehole. Andreas and Heiderose Fischer-Nagel (Carolrhoda Books)

Amazing Fish. Mary Ling (Knopf Books for Young Readers)

Amazing Tropical Birds. Gerald Legg (Knopf Eyewitness Juniors)

Animal Crafts. Worldwide Crafts (series). (Gareth Stevens)

Birds. Wings (series). Patricia Lantier-Sampon (Gareth Stevens)

Dogs: Wild and Domestic. Markus Kappeler (Gareth Stevens)

Fearsome Fish. Steve Parker (Steck-Vaughn)

Fish, Fish, Fish. Georgie Adams (Dial Books for Young Readers)

Frogs. Gail Gibbons (Holiday House)

From Tadpole to Frog. Wendy Pfeffer (Harper Trophy)

Gerbil Pets and Other Small Rodents. (Childrens)

Guinea Pigs. Fiona Henrie (Watts)

Look Out for Turtles! (Harper Collins Children's Books)

My Parrot Eats Baked Beans: Kids Talk About Their Pets. (Whitman)

Rabbits and Hares. Annette Barkhausen and Franz Geiser (Gareth Stevens)

Real Baby Animals (series). Gisela and Siegfried Buck (Gareth Stevens)

Small Cats. Markus Kappeler (Gareth Stevens)

Turtles, Toads and Frogs. George Fichter (Western Publishing)

VIDEOS

Barnyard Babies. (Grunko Films, Inc.)

Paws, Claws, Feathers and Fins. (Kidvidz)

See How They Grow Series - Pets. (Sony)

Spot Goes to the Farm. (Buena Vista Home Video)

PLACES TO WRITE

For more information about animals, contact the following organizations. Be sure to include a self-addressed, stamped envelope.

Canadian Wildlife Federation
2740 Queensview Drive
Ottawa, Ontario K2B 1A2

National Audubon Society
700 Broadway
New York, NY 10003

**The Humane Society of
   the United States**
2100 L Street NW
Washington, D.C. 20037-1598

**Conservation Commission of
   the Northern Territory**
P.O. Box 496
Palmerston, NT 0831 Australia

INDEX

Amazon parrot **3, 13**
Amphibians **22-23**

Birds **11-15**
Black mouse **20**
Brown mouse **20**

Canary **14**
Cats **8-10**
Chinchilla **17**
Cockatoo **11, 13**
Cocker spaniel **6**

Dachshund **4**
Dogs **4-7**

Finch **15**
Fish **24-26**
Frog **23**

Gerbil **20**
Goldfish **24**
Guinea pig **18**
Guppies **25**

Hamster **19**
House cat **8**

Macaw **11, 12**
Mice **19, 20**
Mongolian gerbil **20**

Neon fish **25**

Old English
   sheepdog **7**

Parakeet **3, 11**
Parrot **11-13**

Persian cat **9**
Poodle **5**

Rabbit **16**
Reptile **21**
Rodent **17, 20**

Salamander **22**
Siamese cat **10**
Siamese fighting
   fish **26**

Tortoise **21**
Turtle **21**

White mouse **20**